Africa is a big continent. In the north of Africa is the Sahara Desert. There is lots of sand and it is very hot. There is no rain, so it is difficult for anyone to live there.

Sahara Desert

Africa

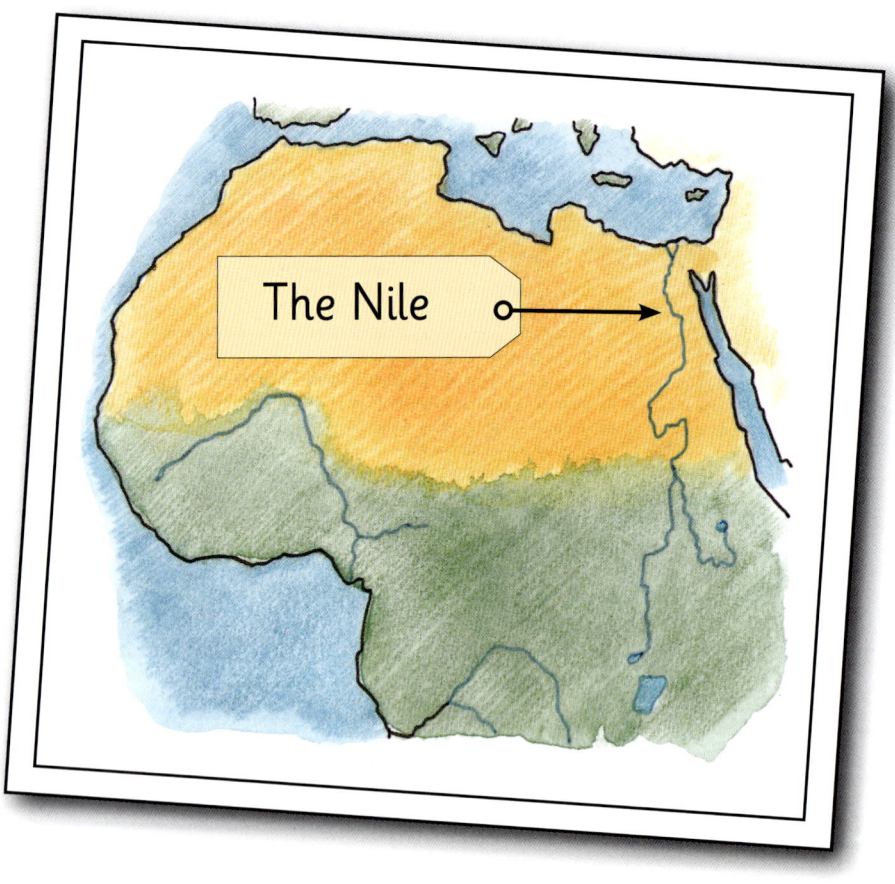

There is a big river in North Africa. This river comes out of the Sahara Desert. It is the biggest river in Africa and it is called the Nile.

From the Nile, the farmers make the land grow crops. The crops grow well and are used for food. Farmers have lived and grown crops next to the Nile for thousands and thousands of years.

crops

The land further away from the Nile does not get wet so crops cannot grow there. It is a desert. All the living things in this part of Africa depend on the River Nile.

desert

Roman army

Some buildings by the Nile are five thousand years old. When an army from Rome came and took the Nile lands, the buildings were already three thousand years old.

But where does the Nile come from? Where does it start? Many years ago, no one knew where it came from. It seemed to come out of the desert.

explorers

Explorers set out to see where it started. They marched up the Nile for a long time. It was hot and there was no rain. They took camels and marched and marched and marched.

They found only sand and desert. When they returned, they said that the Nile must spring up from out of the desert sands. But they had not really found where the River Nile began.

Then, about one hundred and fifty years ago, some men explored far into the middle of Africa. They, too, were looking for the start of the River Nile.

One of these men was called John Speke and, in the end, he was the person who found the start of the Nile.

John Speke

Speke found out that it came from a big lake in the middle of Africa. He named it Lake Victoria. Victoria was the British queen of the time.

It rains a lot around Lake Victoria so it is very lush and green. Where Speke found the start of the Nile, there is now a big dam that makes electric power.

dam

It is hotter in the summer than in the winter. So we would expect rivers to get smaller in the summer because there is less rain. But the Nile is different.

The Nile in winter

In the summer, the Nile gets bigger and spreads out over the land around it. As it does so, it brings earth and mud onto the farmland.

The Nile in summer

This means the farmers can grow crops there. All the farmers depend on the Nile, but for thousands of years no one understood why it is that the Nile gets bigger in the summer.

The reason is because the Nile has to travel a long, long way before it reaches the desert. As it travels along, a second big river joins it from some mountains. In the winter, there is a lot of rain in the mountains.

It is this rain that makes the Nile bigger in the summer. The Nile is so long that it is summer by the time all the rain reaches the Nile in the desert. So this part of the river is at its biggest in the summertime.